GET WRITING
UNDERSTAND
AND NAVIGATE
THE WRITING PROCESS WITH CONFIDENCE

VICTOR KWEGYIR

THE CONFIDENT AUTHOR SERIES:
MASTER THE ART OF WRITING, PUBLISHING, AND STRATEGICALLY
PROMOTING YOUR BOOK FOR SUCCESS

GET WRITING
Understand And Navigate The Writing Process With Confidence

Copyright © 2025 by Victor Kwegyir
All rights reserved.

Unless otherwise indicated, all quotes are taken from *Business 365: Daily Inspiration for Creativity, Innovation and Business Success* by Victor Kwegyir[1]

Publisher
Vike Springs Publishing Ltd.
www.vikesprings.com

First Edition
ISBN-13: 978-1-0686219-6-3- E-book
ISBN-13: 978-1-0686219-7-0- Paperback
ISBN-13: 978-1-0686219-8-7- Audiobook

Printed in the United Kingdom and United States of America

For bulk orders, book writing, coaching and publishing services, as well as bookings for speaking engagements, contact us:
admin@vikesprings.com

LIMIT OF LIABILITY/DISCLAIMER OF WARRANTY

This publication is designed to provide accurate and authoritative information in regard to the subject matter covered. It is sold with the understanding that the publisher and author make no representations or warranties with respect to the completeness of the contents of this work. Neither the publisher nor the author shall be liable for any damages or losses arising herefrom. The fact that an organisation or website is referred to in this work as a citation and/or a potential source of further information does not mean that the author or the publisher endorses the information that the organisation or website may provide, or recommendations it may make. Due to the ever-changing information from the web, internet websites and URLs listed in this work may have changed or been removed. All trademarks or names referenced in this book are the property of their respective owners, and the publisher and author are not associated with any product or vendor mentioned.

DEDICATION

To all our writing, editorial, design, marketing,
distribution and printing teams.

I appreciate you for the amazing work you do.
Vike Springs Publishing has come this far because
of your hard work and commitment.

Let's keep the momentum going, and reach even higher
achievements in helping our authors realise their
writing and publishing goals, one author at a time.

CONTENTS

INTRODUCTION

'Transforming minds globally through words' is a powerful phrase that illustrates the power of the written word. Writing is not just about putting words on paper, it is a creative process that communicates thoughts and emotions, and shares an individual's unique perspective. Writing can transform lives, entertain, inspire, direct, inform, bring revelation, and so much more. Many find that writing is also a journey of self-transformation and personal growth. By expressing our thoughts, we can understand ourselves with more clarity.

Whether you are an aspiring novelist, budding poet, business entrepreneur, minister, or someone who has never thought they could write a book, you will find all you need in this resource to guide you through your writing journey. It covers all aspects of the writing process, from the initial spark of inspiration to the completed manuscript ready for print. You will gain confidence in putting pen to paper – or fingers to keyboard – and as you move towards publication and marketing, know that help is at hand from start to finish.

You may have ideas that you would love to see in print, but just don't know how to begin to write. Or maybe the last time you attempted to write anything was when you were in school, which seems a long time ago. You may have many questions about how to begin, how to build a coherent narrative, or even how you can find time to write when life seems so hectic. These are common concerns for many people who would love to see their book in print, but be encouraged, such a goal is possible to achieve, and it may be easier than you think.

Part I of this book details a ten-day writing plan, where you'll learn how to structure and go about writing your book, and in Part II you will find information about different writing styles, and get tips to help you develop your voice and technique, along with information on the best writing apps to boost your writing ability. Your journey as a writer will be an individual one, but there are pitfalls and challenges that are common to each of us, so you'll find reassurance and stimulation to help you in the process of getting your book ready for publication.

To encourage you, there are also stories from real people who have successfully authored books, explaining the way they managed to do so.

But first, some basics: The ten foundation points shown below give the understanding that you will build upon as you begin to write.

1. Your book marketing starts from the day you decided to write, so think about who your audience is going to be. You will find more information about this vital element of book writing in my book on marketing, *Promote Your Book,* that will help you navigate the marketing maze with confidence.
2. You have a unique voice. You bring your experience and all the elements of who you are into your writing.
3. Find your niche. Whatever you decide to write about your book will fit into a specific category or genre, and you should know from the start where your book belongs, so that it lands in front of your target audience. There are around 50 main genres, and currently Amazon lists about 16,000 sub-genres.
4. Do not aim at perfection. Your aim is to share your story, expertise or information. Professional editing and proofreading are there to perfect it all for you.
5. Whatever you do, write with a purpose with an aim to add value. Never write just to be an author.
6. Writing and publishing a book is an investment. Such a mindset is necessary in order to make wise decisions at each stage in the process.
7. Being an author opens the door for many other opportunities such as public speaking, training programmes, corporate advisory and government-level policy decision-making board roles, expanding your scope of influence, leaving a legacy and gaining financial income.

8. Just like any product out there, books do not sell by themselves.
9. Writing a book helps to establish and authenticate your brand. It confirms your identity.
10. Learn to take rejection well and always be open to feedback.

The following statistics about the book publishing world will help you to focus on what you want to achieve, and help to clarify what you can expect when you enter this exciting and vibrant writing environment.

- Revenue in the books market worldwide is forecasted to reach US$94.98bn in 2025, with an anticipated annual growth rate of 1.58%. [2]
- The self-publishing market is booming with an annual growth rate of 17%, compared to the traditional publishing market of a 1% increase. [3]
- The average sales of self-published books is 250 copies at an average of $4.16. 90% of self-published books sell less than 100 copies. These figures illustrate how important good marketing is. [4]
- Trending book genres are young adult, romance, fantasy, mystery and thriller, historical fiction, science fiction, self-help, and memoirs. Other genres that are doing well are more visual: photo books, graphic novels, and art books. [5]
- eBooks and audiobook sales are skyrocketing, with the demand for print books diminishing. In the UK the demand for audiobooks increased by 17% in 2023 and eBook sales are even higher than audiobooks. [6]

- By 2025, eBooks will generate $17.7 billion in annual revenue around the world.[7]
- Audiobooks are poised for sustained growth, with predictions indicating that audiobook revenues will surpass $5 billion globally by 2025. Increased adoption by younger demographics and improved production quality contribute to this rise.[8]
- The eBook market was estimated to claim over 35% of the global market share by 2025.[9]

This book is one of a three-book series entitled *The Confident Author Series: Master the Art of Writing, Publishing, and Strategically Promoting Your Book for Success* and it covers many aspects of writing, publication and marketing. These books are not meant to be digested in a linear fashion – even when starting your writing journey, you will need to be aware of the next steps, and in particular, marketing should be in place very early on.

Throughout this series you will find quotes from one of my other books *Business 365: Daily Inspiration for Creativity, Innovation and Business Success*. This will encourage and motivate you as you move towards becoming a published author.

You may be one of many who have tried and failed to get your writing into publication, whether through your own circumstances, or being let down by the publication route you attempted. Please don't give up, but be encouraged to look at your situation again, and find a way forward.

"To succeed, you need to find your authenticity, and to become really successful, you need to find your own voice."

PART I
THE TEN DAY PLAN

Ten days, I hear you say! Who can
write a book in ten days?
Well, this is the process I use myself, having
written close to 15 books to date,
and ghostwritten many others.
It's also a process I use when coaching other authors.

*"The process is real! There is work to do,
mistakes to make, risks to take and success
to achieve – if you don't faint first!"*

CHAPTER

1

Take time in Day 1 to get the basics in place. Having a clear understanding of why you want to write and who your audience is will bring grounding to your book idea, instil confidence as you begin, and help you to be successful.

WHY

Explain in detail the reasons why you want to write. What is it you want to achieve? Define your message and consider what writing your book will do for you in the way of your self-image, or your credibility. What will it do for you professionally, or financially? Will it help demonstrate your specialist knowledge or professional development? What will it do for your reader?

The stronger your 'why', the greater the motivation to make it happen, so answer the following questions:

- What will it do for me?
- What will it do for my credibility?
- What will it do for my confidence?
- What will it do for me professionally?
- What will it do for my reader?
- What will it do for me financially?

Are you aiming to entertain readers, explore a certain theme, raise awareness about a particular issue, or something else? How you approach your topic will also be part of your 'Why'. For example, you might wish to include biographical detail but write from a fictional point of view; or you may want to address a current issue where you have a degree of expertise by offering a different perspective.

Think about how important it is for you to get your message across. Your motivation to write will be directly linked to how excited, inspired, or burdened you are by your chosen subject.

Have others ever said to you that you should write a book? Find out what it is that they thought was significant about your message. Can you buy into their belief about you?

In addition, evaluate your 'Why not'. If you think time will be an issue, decide what needs to change so you have more time. If you don't feel your skills are up to writing, then recognise that there are ways around that by getting the right professional support. Don't allow negative thoughts to impact your self-belief. There are readers for every kind of book, so do not think that what you want to say or write about will not be of interest to others.

WHO

> *"I never perfected an invention that I did not think about in terms of the service it might give others... I find out what the world needs, then I proceed to invent."* Thomas Edison

On Day 1 it's also important to decide on who your target audience will be. Define your audience profile and consider the best way to connect with them.

What does the world need from your writing? Think about your likely readership and the range of genres, especially those that are popular, or where your research shows there is a gap in the market. With such a range of genres, decide where you will fit and find out as much as you can about who is reading those books. You can enhance your research by looking at bestsellers in bookshops and online, and ask librarians and booksellers about the genres that are emerging or attracting a lot of interest.

Your ideal reader will gain a sense of value from reading your book so aim to provide quality in-depth information, always geared towards what you understand to be your reader's level of interest or understanding.

If you are considering a children's book, your research should also look at the adults who will be purchasing the book to read to the child. Children's books should fit into a defined age range, and the length of the book and the vocabulary will differ according to age. For example, board books are for 0-3 year-old children. They are less than 300 words in length, contain a lot of pictures and simple words, often rhyming. In contrast, books for young adults, aged 12 plus, are at the other end of the spectrum, are 45-80,000 words in length and use a wide range of vocabulary.

Be aware of the different themes that appeal to teens, young adults, and older readers and think about where to target your writing. For example, children are often interested in books about friendships, families, emotions and behaviour; whereas young adults may be keen to explore issues that help them with relationships and understanding their own self-concept. They often explore themes of morality.

In creating a clear reader profile, you will also need to understand where your book will be listed. The category of your book placement needs to be precise.

For example, a love story that is also a travelog may be difficult to place, or a book about the best way to run a business will not be read by your target audience if it is too restrictive in the type of business it describes.

Questions you can ask yourself are:

- Who will read my book?
- Where will they find my book?
- How will it help them/inspire them/change them?
- What do I want them to say about my book to their family, friends and work colleagues?

> *"The value of a question is in the answer it generates. Give it a bit more thought if you expect the right answer."*

CHAPTER

2

Your book title will capture the attention of your readers and invite them to find out more. The contents will need to be 'what it says on the tin', although the title can also be intriguing or excite curiosity. As you think about your title, look at the genre of book you are planning to write, and notice the titles that grab your attention, as these will probably be in line with the style of writing you will produce. To help you further, online title generators can offer suggestions when you enter details of your writing.

If you can't think of a suitable title, describe what you would like the title to convey to your audience, including any subtitle or tagline. This will help clarify your thinking.

The title you choose can also reflect your brand and link in to future publications, or other marketing. Your book title will also affect sales, and needs to stand out and be different from other publications.

A working title is a useful way to start – you can always amend it when your book is written, and when you understand more about the impact of the message or story that you have created.

A note of caution: once you decide on your title, do check that there are not any other books that share the same title, as this can be very confusing for the reader, who may decide to buy your book but instead buy a different book that has the same wording on the cover.

CHAPTER HEADINGS AND SUB-HEADINGS

Whether you are writing fiction or non-fiction, you will need a clear structure. Begin by mapping out the chapters and chapter headings, then write a list or short description of what you consider needs to be captured under each chapter with sub-headings where necessary. You will think about how you will tell your story and develop the writing from a strong and attention-grabbing beginning to a clear conclusion. There is no need at this stage to write anything in detail, but make sure to include all aspects of the message you want to communicate.

Different genres have different structures, so think about how you want your story to develop. Do you start at the beginning, or refer to the beginning later on in the book? Decide if your book, whether fiction or non-fiction, will end with the ending, or leave the reader wanting to read more of what you are writing about.

If you are writing fiction, think about your characters and how they will develop in your story. Draft descriptions of each character using both visual and personality words. What will they look like at the end of your story? Have a clear picture in your mind of any mannerisms or other memorable traits that they should have.

For non-fiction, think about how you will develop your theme and define what needs to be included at what particular point of your narrative.

As with your title, the chapters and sub-headings may change as you begin to write and allow the process to develop, but having a clear structure from the start will help to keep you focussed and know that you have a solid framework that will keep things on track.

> *"Planning gives birth to strategy. Without a plan there is no strategy, and without strategy there is no effective and efficient execution."*

CHAPTER

3

It's time! You've been burning to get your ideas down on paper, and the moment is here where you can dedicate the next five days to writing. The first thing you need to do is schedule your time. It's very easy to become distracted and all too soon discouragement can set in, so find a comfortable writing environment where you can concentrate and focus. Writing takes self-discipline, but brings a sense of achievement when you realise how well you are progressing.

You have your structure. Now set your goals of what you will achieve in each time frame you set, by dividing the number of chapters over the five days. If you feel overwhelmed by the size of the task, focus on just one chapter or sub-heading at a time.

For non-fiction, it helps to read about your subject for about an hour before beginning to write each day, and for fiction, it can help to envisage your character from the end of your story and work backwards.

Don't worry too much about getting it all right on your first draft. Just get the words out in written form, and know it can be reviewed at a later date. There are also opportunities for getting editorial development advice and general editing as you proceed. Your writing style should be natural for you as it will convey authenticity. Don't try to write like other people, but do explore how others have written in the same genre, as this will stimulate your creativity. What level of vocabulary will your target reader have? Consider how teen reads are written differently, or how books that are aimed towards academia are written.

Keep reminding yourself **why** you are writing, **who** your audience is, and review the layout of your book. Any areas that need more development or that you are stuck on can be revisited at a later date, so highlight those areas and move on.

"One of the greatest discoveries in life is knowing who you are, what you've been created for and what it takes to accomplish it."

GETTING STUCK

Prepare to get stuck at some point! Many people hit blocks in their writing, or become discouraged. Take regular breaks and switch off. Allow things to settle and discover how new aspects of your writing will come to mind from your subconscious even as you focus on something else, and inspiration can re-emerge.

Take time to look again at your structure and plan, do some research, read through what you have done so far, read through this book, and encourage yourself. Re-design your goals and expectations if you need to.

You may find that you need a different working environment, or need to talk it through with someone who can give constructive guidance and help you see where you should change direction. You can also reach out or consider signing up to one of my company's writing coaching workshops, one-to-one writing coaching, ghost writing or developmental writing services at this stage, if not earlier.

Setbacks are opportunities to reflect and to grow in understanding, so don't let such roadblocks knock you off course.

Once you have re-grouped, you will be able to focus again, return to your plan, and recommit to the self-discipline of writing. Remember that many people think they can write, but never get further than thinking about it – what you are doing is more than that, and if you persevere you will achieve the prize.

"Get your thinking right, and the rest is history."

CHAPTER

4

Spend some time reviewing what you have done, and re-visit your **why** and **who**. This will maintain motivation and keep you from becoming mired down in detail that is not part of your plan.

For fiction, go over your story to see if there are areas you can enrich, or characters that need to improve or need to have stronger integration with the story. For non-fiction, look again at your initial notes and research, making sure that your facts are being communicated clearly and accurately. Read over all chapters and do any additional research for all the marked places in the book you highlighted earlier.

Try to identify how quickly your reader will engage with your message. If your reasons for writing your book or other introductory information is too lengthy, will they disengage before getting to the meat of your writing?

It's tempting to rush to completion, but like a fine wine, allow your book to mature and settle. Keep reviewing and editing, be prepared to delete and refine, look out for words that are repeated, and of course, use your spell check. It's a good exercise to rewrite a certain section as if you are writing it for the first time, and then compare the different versions. Make sure you are meeting the chapter heading and sub-heading descriptions, and that there is a sense of pacing and clarity.

Get as much feedback as you can – whether from professionals or people you trust. Consider what they say, and edit again if necessary. In all this appreciate the significant role of the professional editor when you submit your manuscript to us for publishing. Our experienced professional editors will perfect your work to meet the highest international standards.

RESEARCH, RESEARCH, RESEARCH

Incorporating research into your writing process will enhance the quality and impact of your book, and it will be more engaging, credible and memorable for your readers.

Whatever you choose to write about, whether fiction or non-fiction, you will need to be accurate. Memory is fallible, so check everything, ensuring that you have all the correct facts.

Your writing will sound authentic when you can demonstrate that you have a thorough knowledge of what you are talking about. Alternatively, if there's any discord or discrepancy in your story you will lose the reader and leave them frustrated. Your research will help you to bring into play facts that may not be generally well-known, and this can bring depth to your story.

Some authors travel to the area they wish to write about, so their words can describe the situation in a way that shows actual knowledge. Other authors consult experts in order to gain specialised knowledge, such as police procedures.

Research can also open up new areas that you can include in your writing. This may mean a new plot direction in fiction writing, or a widening of the scope of the non-fiction subject you are addressing.

In addition, writing what is accurate and true protects from libel claims, which is where someone claims their reputation has been damaged by what you wrote.

If you are writing non-fiction, your sources for information should be cited; but even for fiction, keeping a record of your research is a useful habit to get into.

"Working hard still counts. Just add strategy and working smart to it if you genuinely want to become successful."

CHAPTER

5

Again, revisit your **why** and **who**, and review your outline. Read over your work and fill in any gaps that still need your input. Think about how you can enrich your writing, whether fiction or non-fiction, so that your message or story becomes stronger.

Now write your conclusion, which should bring together all the points you want to communicate, and complete your story, leaving your reader with a clear idea of what you would like them to know, feel, or action.

Some questions you might want to ask around your conclusion:

- What will my readers take away?
- What will encourage them?
- What will illuminate and bring increased knowledge?

- What will inspire them?
- What will challenge them?
- What will they tell their family, friends, or work colleagues about how the book has impacted them?
- Do the answers to these questions fit my reader profile?

Again, go back to your **why** and **who** and look at your written conclusion in the light of your original thoughts.

EACH PERSON'S WRITING PROCESS IS DIFFERENT

The above is general advice, but each person differs in the way they proceed. Some hit setbacks and the project will go on hold for a long time, others become more and more inspired as they write, and find the process fits very well into the ten-day structure.

Some writers will have no structure in mind, but instead just let the story flow. Yet others will use earlier writing and develop it into a longer narrative.

You might think that everyone writes from the beginning of their book through to the end, but that's not the case, as some people write sections about certain aspects of their story, and then piece it all together towards the end of their writing. You might also believe that everyone uses electronic means to write their manuscripts, but there are also many who prefer to write by hand, and others who dictate their books that are then transcribed. Just focus on getting the words out there – whether onto paper, your computer screen or in audio form which is then transcribed.

You can always record what you want to write (as humans tend to speak two to three times faster than typing or writing) and send it to us to transcribe, edit and manage the entire publishing process for you. This can save significant time in helping you to get your story or message out.

Don't feel too uneasy if the way you write doesn't fit into how other people think you should be doing it. Whatever works for you, and brings out your creativity and enthusiasm, is the right way! The beautiful thing about writing books is the amazing variety of ideas and the many different ways of inspiring others through words.

"Your uniqueness is a potentially outstanding ability the world is yet to see."

CHAPTER

6

Read your book again and think about how it lines up with your aims at the start. Check the facts you are presenting, review your characters (for fiction) and story development. Make sure you have included all you wanted to when you first decided on your chapter headings and sub-headings.

Remember that your writing doesn't have to be perfect. Professional editors and writers can provide developmental editing, copyediting, and ghostwriting to help you get your writing to the point where it is ready to go to print. There are also some very good writing apps, and these are detailed in Part II.

GHOSTWRITING

Perhaps you have an idea, a great plot, or have a structure but there are gaps in your knowledge that means you can't write with enough authority about the subject. Or maybe you are at a place in your life where you know you can't give your book idea the attention it deserves.

There are many reasons why people use a ghostwriter. Many great people with great ideas are not necessarily good authors. A ghostwriter can take your ideas and communicate them using their writing expertise, which is a great combination and leads to a quality product.

A ghostwriter can save you time and money and alleviate the stress that you might encounter if you try to write yourself. And you can use this option to develop your goal of becoming a published author.

ARTIFICIAL INTELLIGENCE (AI) WRITING

This option is becoming more popular in helping people develop their thoughts into coherent narrative. Please remember it is a computer-generated voice, and it may not be accurate, as it only generates what is fed into it.

It may help to order your thoughts using this process, but you should still 'make it your own' by ensuring that you maintain your writing style, and convey your own understanding of the subject you are writing about.

Note: There is an inherent risk with a lot of copyright issues coming up in the courts in these early stages of using AI. Until such a time that the laws are clearly established you should remain very cautious in using AI tools to write a book.

"Want to save a lot of money, stress and time?
Think of value instead of cost when working with a coach."

PART II
MORE WRITING TIPS

Part II provides some information about writing styles, along with information about other help that's available in your quest to become a published author.

You can also learn about some great authors and their writing process.

"Irrespective of the challenges, the process will become exciting if the destination is real enough to you!"

CHAPTER

7

Some information about different writing styles will help you decide the best way to express your thoughts in your chosen genre. A combination of these will help to engage your readers.

Consider the base sentence of 'the sun shone this morning', and discover how different styles can change the tone.

- Descriptive writing paints a picture with words and is used most in travel writing, poetry or fiction.

Example: The golden sun burst its radiance upon the beautiful morning, bringing light to all.

- Narrative writing tells a story and as you might expect is used in novels, short stories, and autobiographies.

Example: As the day began, people in the household began to stir, drawing the curtains back to reveal the sun shining brightly as the world awakened. But little did they know that by the time afternoon arrived, darkness would overtake the earth.

- Journalistic writing reports news and facts, so it is concise and objective.

Example: The city experienced bright sunshine this morning, which provided a welcome change from recent cloudy days. Parks and outdoor cafes were thronged with people enjoying the pleasant weather.

- Expository writing is similar to journalistic in that it presents facts, statistics and examples. It is used in academic writing and writing that conveys information or instructs.

Example: The sun rises earlier in the summer months in the Northern Hemisphere because the earth is tilted towards the sun, which results in more direct sunlight and a longer day. This is why the sun appears to rise earlier in the morning.

- Technical writing will be used in manuals and guides. It addresses complex issues in a clear way, so that direction can be followed easily.

Example: Sunrise at 6.45am indicated an increased recorded intensity of sunlight, contributing to a rapid rise in ambient temperature from 18° to 22°C within the first hour of daylight.

- Persuasive writing is, as the name conveys, a way of writing to persuade the reader to adopt your point of view. It uses evidence and emotional appeals.

Example: You should make a point of noticing when you wake up to a sunny day, as this will improve your mood and help you start the day with positivity.

- Compare and contrast is a style that shows similarities and differences between two or more things being compared. It helps readers understand how things relate and connect with each other.

Example: This morning's weather offered a marked change from the gloomy and overcast mornings we have experienced in the past week. Today the sun shone warmly, bringing light to the day, as opposed to the dull starts we have had recently.

- Reflective writing or personal writing is a way of processing experience. This style of writing includes diaries, journals, and blog posts.

Example: When I see the sun shining in the morning, my heart begins to sing, and I feel energised and up-beat.

It is not just about writing style – each of these styles will include differing vocabularies, length of sentences, length of paragraphs and layout. You may find that once you have put your book together, you decide to use a professional to make sure you hit the right tone and choose the right style.

> *"It is only by admiring and aiming for higher standards that we become successful."*

CHAPTER

8

FICTION

Whether writing adult fiction, teen reads, sci-fi, children's stories or other fiction, there are some distinct areas to focus on, some of which are listed below:

- Developing a strong plot is a vital part of telling a compelling story. You will need to engage your reader from the start, and the story needs to be woven together in a way that has pace and balance to keep your reader's attention.
- Understand the conflict you are trying to convey, as this will build drama. This could be an internal conflict that your main character struggles with, or conflict with another character.
- Use descriptive words carefully. Overuse comes across as amateur, and with underuse you are left with a dry and uninspiring narrative.

- When developing your characters, determine how you want them to be at the end of your story then think about how you want them to progress to that point. Give them depth of personality and use a clear visual description.
- Situate your characters and your story in an environment that feels real and compelling.
- Take care not to put your characters in situations that are not age-appropriate, for example introducing an 85-year-old woman to your story, and later referring to her sprinting down the road.
- Similarly, your story should sound authentic. It needs to reflect the cultural environment where it is situated.
- Your dialogue will bring your characters alive. They need to have distinctive tones and vocabulary. Avoid them stating the obvious, talking in big chunks, saying each other's names too much, or including too many overly descriptive dialogue tags.
- What do you want your story to do? Engage, excite, entertain … ? Keep going back to your aims and check that your writing is achieving these aims, whether overtly or with subtle nudges to your reader.

"You are never short of passion when you are an original."

NON-FICTION

Any non-fiction book requires the writer to know what they are writing about! Whether it is a biography, a book about a specific niche topic, or an historical account, here are some general tips:

- You need to write clearly, and engage your readers from the start so that they will identify with your ideas and understand your interest and passion for the subject.
- As previously stated, research your topic thoroughly.
- Using personal examples, or accounts from other people, will add human interest.
- Forewords, introductions and clear conclusions will put your writing into context. The reader will know about you, what you want to convey, and what you want them to take with them when they finish.
- Be clear and concise – don't ramble or go off at a tangent.
- You need to show where you get your information from through footnotes or endnotes or a list of references. You can also list further reading in a bibliography.
- Depending on your subject, you can include photographs, maps, graphs and other visuals that will help convey your message in more depth.
- Again, depending on what you are writing about, you may wish to include questions or

reflexive practices for your reader, so they can enhance their own experience of your writing.

• Be aware of elements of your writing that may date, or be superseded by events. To counteract this, you may wish to focus on using statements and information that is general and will not date.

POINTS OF VIEW (POV)

Whether writing non-fiction or fiction, spend some time considering the position you are writing from, as the perspective you choose can dramatically change the impact of your book. Explore writing from different points of view to get a better understanding of the impact your writing will have and how it will bring clarity, authority, credibility, and also get your reader to identify and agree with what you are saying.

In brief, using a first-person POV in **non-fiction writing** will convey a personal tone, but using a third-person approach is more objective. For example, an autobiography that is written in third person leaves the reader wondering what the author is actually feeling – it is too detached from the actual story and loses authenticity. Consider your reader when choosing your POV – academic readers will prefer a neutral or authoritative POV that presents information indicating the writer is an expert, whereas general readers will respond to a conversational tone, which may include personal opinion.

Choosing the right POV for **fiction writing** is a very powerful tool, as it can either bring characters to life or leave the reader feeling disinterested. The narrator may be a participant in the story, which will mean using the first person singular, 'I'. It's a powerful way of telling a story, but is limited to only recounting what the narrator experiences themself. First person plural describes the experiences of a group of people, using 'we', but this can become tedious and lose impact. Third person singular refers to the main character as 'he' and gives a close understanding of the character but can also provide wider perspective that the character himself doesn't have. Third person omniscient is a term that describes the narrator's ability to describe any character's perspective and any events from an all-encompassing and all-knowing viewpoint. You may find you want to limit the narrator's POV by using first person singular or first person plural, as that can create mystery and leave the reader wanting to discover more; or alternatively use omniscience to add vital information to your plot, so the reader will feel they know more about the situation than the characters they are following.

"It stands to reason that when you enjoy what you do, it fuels your quest to become better at it, and to deliver excellence."

CHAPTER

9

As you will have recognised, the publishing business is booming with the rise in self- and hybrid-publishing, which means that anyone and everyone can write, and that includes you!

To help with this writing boom, a number of online apps are available, offering different levels of support. They also vary in cost. 18 of these are detailed below.

SCRIVENER[10]

A scrivener or scribe was someone who wrote letters and documents for others, and this app is designed to help you write. It offers a place to store all your ideas and research, as well as to write your manuscript, and tracks your writing goals to help keep you focused.

ULYSSES[11]

This is an app for Mac, iPad and iPhone, and as well as your actual manuscript, offers areas to store your ideas, areas that are still being developed, and wording you have scrapped. It has a built-in editing and proofreading function, and makes it easy to proceed to print.

PLOTTR[12]

Plottr helps you develop timelines and plots, character development and other elements of your story. It can organise and bring clarity, so you can make sure your plot is solid and there are no unaddressed elements. It can export to Word, and import from Scrivener and Snowflake Pro.

SNOWFLAKE PRO[13]

This app applies the snowflake method for fiction writing, helping authors develop a clear, well-structured story framework. It also helps you to write a book proposal based on your material.

IA WRITER[14]

iA Writer helps track what you have written and what has come from other sources. It offers links between your thoughts, suggesting other areas to consider, along with clear formatting and a syntax highlight feature which advises ways you can improve the words and phrases you are using.

YWRITER[15]

This free app has been commended as best for scene-based writing, helping to organise chapters, characters, and scenes with ease, and offering analysis of metadata from your writing into charts and tables so you can assess exactly what you are writing about.

STORYIST[16]

Storyist is used for screenplays and novels, and formats as you write. You can have comments, images, headers, footers, and style sheets; and ideas for plot and characters are stored on 'index cards' that can be shown alongside your writing.

FINAL DRAFT[17]

This app helps budding screenwriters, with building blocks and outlines that you can add to in order to create your movie or TV script.

GRAMMARLY[18]

Grammarly describes itself as an AI writing partner that helps you find the words you need – to write that tricky email, to get your point across, to keep your work moving. It helps with drafting, re-writing, changing tone, and keeping writers 'on-brand'.

PROWRITINGAID[19]

This app provides critique, suggests improvements to make the story more dynamic, fixes common writing mistakes and eliminates weak words. It expands on your writing, using AI.

HEMINGWAY EDITOR[20]

This app will highlight sentences that need to be written in simpler form, and grades your writing as you type, showing readability, grammar and spelling issues, and words that have simpler alternatives.

READABLE[21]

Similarly, Readable will analyse your writing and show you how to improve it.

NATURALREADER[22]

This app will take written material and convert it into the spoken word. You can select the type of voice you want. It also offers multi-lingual voices for a range of different languages.

FREEDOM[23]

This app is designed to eliminate distractions, so that you can focus on your writing. You can choose which websites and apps you want to block while you write, and for how long, and you can block these on all your devices so you don't get distracted by call alerts, etc.

EVERNOTE[24]

Evernote can sync over all your devices and is a storage repository for all your ideas, quotes, audio or image inspiration. Using it will save you hunting through your history or emails for that information that you need but can't now locate.

REEDSY PROMPTS[25]

This is a website that encourages writers to develop their creativity by providing 'prompts' for storytelling ideas. It hosts a weekly short story competition, and also offers other advice to get people writing regularly.

NOVELIZE[26]

As the name says, Novelize is an app to help you write a novel. It claims to be a writing partner, offering outline, write and organise modes. It interfaces with Grammarly and ProWritingAid for spelling and grammar support. It also helps you maintain your word count goals as you write.

REEDSY BOOK EDITOR[27]

This is a free tool used for book production, as it formats and applies styles as you write, and readies your writing so it can go directly to print.

"Entrepreneurs are self-motivators and hardworking!"

CHAPTER
10

The parts of a book are often called front matter, main text and end matter. In the **front matter** (before the main text) you will find the title page and the copyright page, followed by some or all of the following: dedication, foreword, preface, acknowledgements and lists of illustrations, abbreviations and other significant content. There may also be an epigraph.

With regards to **end matter**, depending on the nature of your book, you may include an appendix, a glossary, endnotes, bibliography or references, notes on contributors or an index.

These headings may not necessarily be in the order shown above, and further explanation of some of these sections is shown below.

FRONT MATTER

Dedication. This is a short personal tribute made by the author – it may refer to why the book was written or the reasons why the book was dedicated to that person or group.

Foreword. The foreword is written by someone other than the author in order to recommend the book, and often details the relationship between the author and the person writing the foreword.

Preface. This is different to an introduction, in that it sets out the scope of the work and puts it in context. A preface can also include brief acknowledgements in place of a separate acknowledgement section.

Acknowledgements. The acknowledgements page lists those who have been helpful or inspirational to the writer in creating the book.

Epigraph. An epigraph is a relevant quotation, phrase or poem that is set on a separate page. It introduces the work, setting the scene or inviting thoughtful consideration. Epigraphs can also be placed throughout a book at the beginning (or end) of chapters or different sections.

END MATTER

Appendix. An appendix contains further information that doesn't sit well within the main narrative, but is useful additional content.

Glossary. An alphabetical list of terms used with explanations of what they mean.

Endnotes. Endnotes are an alternative form of footnotes, where it's unnecessary to have the reference in the main text.

Bibliography. This is a list of works referred to or information for further reading. Authors are listed alphabetically.

References. A reference list is similar to a bibliography, but only contains information on work cited in the text (as opposed to further reading or other information).

Index. This section is usually included in more detailed publications and lists the pages where certain topics are referred to in the book.

> *"The human mind is unbelievably rich with great ideas and possibilities. Employ it, feed it, challenge it, and it will work wonders for you."*

CHAPTER
11

WRITING GROUPS

Writing can sometimes feel quite a solitary business, but budding authors can obtain encouragement, friendship, and information from writing groups. These can often be found locally, but if you don't have anything suitable near to you, there are also a number of writing groups online where you can receive similar support.

A writing group can help you improve writing skills, or try new styles. Such groups can provide feedback and boost confidence, and you can learn from how others have proceeded to print and their success (or failure) in their marketing strategy.

Writing workshops and one-to-one writing coaching can also provide encouragement, inspiration and a new perspective. There are numerous aspiring authors who have appreciated this input, which I have provided over many years.

SOME FAMOUS WRITERS AND THEIR PROCESS

Generally, writers have clear habits and routines. Rather than wait for inspiration to strike, they discipline themselves to a hard grind.

Like many others, the author Salman Rushdie writes at the beginning of the day avoiding distractions. He writes without editing initially, focusing only on getting his thoughts out onto paper. Before I stumbled on how he writes, this was and is still my preferred approach in most of my writing. Knowing that he approaches his writing in a similar way gave me confidence and spurred me on in my writing journey.

Ernest Hemingway famously said that the art of writing is the art of applying the seat of the pants to the seat of the chair.

Many writers push themselves physically too. Their routine is not just making time and space for writing, but also ensuring that they exercise, as they find that helps them to also work hard mentally. One writer, A.J. Jacobs, when writing his book *Drop Dead Healthy*[28], recognised the importance of physical exercise, and so he put his computer on a treadmill and worked as he exercised. He says, "It took me about 1,200 miles to write my book." This author also recommends setting aside time to just generate ideas – even if most of them don't see the light of day, there will be some that are inspirational.

Jodi Picoult is a No.1 New York Times bestselling author. She stresses the importance of getting words on paper, even if it isn't the best writing. She maintains that you can't edit a blank page, but you can always edit writing that you think is substandard. E.B. White, who has authored 20 books of prose and poetry, is quoted as saying, "A writer who waits for ideal conditions under which to work will die without putting a word on paper."

Maya Angelou, author and poet, had a very precise routine, renting a hotel room just to write. She said, "Easy reading is damn hard writing. But if it's right, it's easy. It's the other way round, too. If it's slovenly written, then it's hard to read. It doesn't give the reader what the careful writer can give the reader."

We can take inspiration from these literary giants, but can also recognise the struggles and difficulties that they experience in order to get their books written. As you write, know the routine that suits you best, and be encouraged to push through any obstacles that present.

"If you don't love what you do, you wear out in no time."

CONCLUSION
THE NEXT STEP

This book has set out information about the writing process that will have given you confidence as you begin your journey towards becoming a published author. Although there are many ways to get support and advice with your writing, it is also important to recognise that you will need to be committed to the long term, and this is where your vision for your book is so important, as it will fuel your motivation and keep you persevering if you hit difficulties and setbacks. Of course, no-one knows for sure how many writers start to write and never finish, but the estimates for this are very high, with some saying 97%. So be warned – many don't make it, but the process of writing a book and getting it published and sold, is a great accomplishment and worth pursuing.

The team at Vike Springs offers a wealth of experience from proven professionals with a cumulative experience of over 105 years. Many of us have authored books ourselves, and we always deliver beyond our customers' expectations. We are truly international, having published for clients from almost every continent, and we offer fast turnaround times without compromising on quality. We publish worldwide in the four main formats – eBook, paperback, hardback and audiobook.

You may have considered the option of ghostwriting, and we can provide further details of the process if you wish to pursue this option.

You may also be interested to know that we can arrange for transcription of recorded messages or speeches into electronic or written format.

Book translation is also an option.

Vike Springs Publications are at hand to answer any questions you have, and to help you to get your published book to your audience. To add to your toolkit of knowledge, read the other books in this series: *Get Published* and *Promote your Book*; and please do get in touch with us to find out more about how we can meet your specific requirements. A full list of our range of services is shown in Appendix 1.

APPENDIX 1
STANDARD BOOK PUBLISHING PROPOSAL

Dear Author,

Thank you very much for your interest in our services.

Vike Springs Publishing Ltd. is an international publishing house based in London, United Kingdom, and a proud member of **IBPA** (Independent Book Publishers Association) **USA**. As a Publishing House we are driven by the vision to work with authors in publishing world-class quality books and giving them maximum exposure around the globe. We are confident that with our team of industry professionals we can work with you to help you share your work, expertise, and knowledge with the global community.

Our **Comprehensive Self-Publishing** packages, we believe, would be of great benefit to you. From comprehensive editorial and proofreading services, custom interior layout and cover design, standout author branding packages to effective marketing and promotion packages, these services have been put together to afford you the flexibility to choose the one that meets your unique needs. You will also enjoy the freedom of choosing the sale price and earn 100% of your royalties received from all major bookseller platforms worldwide.

COMPREHENSIVE SELF-PUBLISHING PACKAGES

Standard Packages	Silver	Gold	Platinum
ISBN Assignment & UPC Barcode	✓	✓	✓
Books in Print Registration	✓	✓	✓
Editorial Assessment	✓	✓	✓
Content Editing, Copyediting & Plagiarism Checks	✓	✓	✓
Proofreading	✓	✓	✓
Custom Book Interior Layout Design	✓	✓	✓
Custom Book Cover Design with 3D copies	✓	✓	✓
E-Book Formatting & Publishing	✓	✓	✓
Barnes & Noble "Read Instantly"	✓	✓	✓
One-on-One Support & S Media Marketing Advice	✓	✓	✓
Amazon "Look Inside" and Google Preview	✓	✓	✓
Worldwide Book Distribution	✓	✓	✓
Paperback and Hardback Publishing	✓	✓	✓
FREE Complimentary Author Paperback Copies *	TBC	TBC	TBC
Author Brand Promo (Electronic Flyer & Posters)	—	✓	✓
Social Media Intro Promo Launch	—	✓	✓
Audiobook Production & Publishing	—	—	✓
Marketing & Promotion	—	—	✓

Reach out to us for our two-page publishing proposal for your consideration.

We also offer **ghostwriting services**, and **developmental writing services**. Each of these options provide a great opportunity to get all your ideas and thoughts set out professionally, in a way that can have the maximum impact on your intended audience.

An added benefit of our services is helping you publish your book on all global book platforms, such as, **Amazon global**, **Barnes and Noble**, **Ingram**, **Kindle**, **Smashwords**, **Draft2Digital**, **Apple iBooks**, **Gardners & Extended Retailer**, **Odilo**, **WHSmith (Kobo)**, **Scribd**, **Baker & Taylor**, **Tolino**, **OverDrive**, **Bibliotheca**, **Palace Marketplace**, **Vivlio**, **Borrowbox**, **Everand**, **Fable**, **Hoopla**, **public libraries**, with direct access to **Independent Bookstore buyers** in the **USA**, **North America** and **Europe**, and many more, in both eBook, paperback, hardback and audiobook formats, as well as providing world class quality book printing services, delivered on time to your chosen address.

Your book would also be made available on the global book inventory system, accessed by independent booksellers, libraries, and wholesale book buyers around the world.

We would love to hear from you on how we can work with you to make your work available to the wider global community. We hope you find your best fit package from our full range of packages for your consideration. If not, we would be more than glad to deliver a custom package that meets your requirements.
Hope to hear from you soon.
Thank you.

APPENDIX 2

AUTHOR REVIEWS

"I would like to thank Vike Springs Publishing for all of their helpful advice, support and assistance in bringing my book to life ... they have been so patient with me. I would highly recommend them." **Don Scott,** Author of *You are An Overcomer & Workbook. London - UK*

"A friend recommended Vike Springs ... Their contribution was immense and enormous. They assist you to put out your message in a simplified way by reaching your target audience..." **Bishop Dr. Gabriel Donkor,** Author of *I Did It By Prayer* and *The 21ˢᵗ Century Generals. New York - USA*

"My son and I are happy with the customer service and guidance received from Vike Spring Publishing. The finished book looked exactly how we envisioned it to be. We would recommend their services ... Vike Springs Publishing is one of the few publishers that launch your book on multiple platforms." **Krysta Williams & Nathaniel Dawkins,** Authors of *Nathaniel's 1st Day of School. Kingston - Jamaica*

"God gives us assignments to execute for him. But He aligns people along that journey to help us execute those mandates. ... He orchestrated ... Vike Springs Publishing ... to have *'The Cruxes'* published. ... From the start to finish, they exhibited professionalism, excellence, speed and delivery ... Forever grateful" **Harriet Oppong,** Author of *The Cruxes: Getting to the Heart of What's Important. Accra - Ghana*

"... Thank you for invaluable advice, patience understanding and for taking time to edit the manuscript. You were always on hand to clarify anything about the process that I did not understand. Nothing was too little or big for you..." **Dr. Esther Fenty,** Author of *Baby Nathaniel – Growing in Church. London - UK*

"My overall experience of working with Vike Springs Publishers has been of top standard. No challenges were too much trouble...The editorial team were fantastic in all they did. You have done well beyond my expectations. Thank you." **Elder Joseph Asuquo,** Author of *From Questions to Applications. London – UK*

APPENDIX 3

"The session was very reassuring and encouraging to get started in writing immediately."
Florence, UK

"The book writing workshop was timely for me. I was in doubt about booking onto the seminar but really pleased that I did. It was informative and provided the confidence I needed to continue exploring the ideas for my book as a non-writer. Thanks Victor."
Deidrea, UK

"The book writing workshop was enlightening. It gave me a great overview of how to get my book written and I left the workshop with the confidence I need to get started. Thank you for running it."
Catherine, Ghana

"The book writing workshop was a great refresher and helping motivate me to complete my books … I will be interested in publishing with your company."
Vonetta, USA

ENDNOTES

1   Kwegyir, V. Business *365: Daily Inspiration for Creativity, Innovation and Business Success.* Vike Springs Publishing Ltd (23 July 2020)

2   Statista.com/Market Insights/Books Worldwide. https://www.statista.com/outlook/amo/media/books/worldwide#:~:text=Revenue%20in%20the%20Books%20market,US%2499.47bn%20by%202029.

3   Blurb Blog. *Book Trends to Look for in 2024.* https://www.blurb.com/blog/book-publishing-trends/#:~:text=Of%20these%2C%20young%20adult%2C%20romance,popular%20book%20genres%20in%202024..

4   Blurb Blog.*Ibid.*

5   Blurb Blog.*Ibid.*

6   Exploding Topics. *11 Top Publishing Trends 2024.* https://explodingtopics.com/blog/publishing-trends

7   Statista.com/ Forecast of epublishing Revenue/ https://www.statista.com/forecasts/456813/epublishing-revenue-in-the-world-forecast

8   Scottmax. *49 Book Industry Statistics To Know* https://scottmax.com/book-industry-statistics-to-know/#General_Book_Industry_Statistics

9   Scottmax. *Ibid.*

10   Scrivener https://scrivener.app/

11   Ulysses https://ulysses.app/

12   Plottr https://plottr.com/

13   Snowflake Pro https://www.advancedfictionwriting.com/product/snowflake-pro-software-link/

14   iAWriter https://ia.net/writer

15   yWriter https://www.spacejock.com/yWriter.html

16   Storyist https://storyist.com/

17   Final Draft https://www.finaldraft.com/

18   Grammarly https://www.grammarly.com/

19   ProWriting Aid https://prowritingaid.com/

20   Hemingway Editor https://hemingwayapp.com/

21   Readable https://readable.app/en

22   Natural Reader https://www.naturalreaders.com/

23   Freedom https://freedom.to/

24   Evernote https://evernote.com/

25   Reedsy Prompts https://blog.reedsy.com/creative-writing-prompts/

26   Novelize https://www.getnovelize.com/

27   Reedsy Book Editor https://reedsy.com/write-a-book/

28   Jacobs, A.J., *Drop Dead Healthy: One Man's Humble Quest for Bodily Perfection.* Simon & Schuster (10 April 2012)

www.ingramcontent.com/pod-product-compliance
Lightning Source LLC
Chambersburg PA
CBHW071630040426
42452CB00009B/1570